Sergeant Jen says

By Sergeant Jennefer Resko

www.asksergeantjen.com

Sergeant Jen Says...Let's Talk about Strangers

Copyright© 2012 Ask Sergeant Jen

All rights reserved. No part of this publication may be reproduced, stored in any retrieval system, or transmitted in any form or by any means, mechanical, photocopying, recording, or otherwise, without permission in writing from the author, except by a reviewer, who may quote brief passages in a review to be printed in a magazine or newspaper.

Manufactured in the United States of America.

ISBN-13: 978-0615674100 (AskSergeantJen)
ISBN-10: 0615674100

Illustrations created by: "Indah" (Indonesia).

All illustrations are owned by the 3-15 Documentation Group, LLC, Parent company of Ask Sergeant Jen.

DISCLAIMER: Nothing in this book is the direct teachings of the Miami-Dade Police Department, but instead is a conglomerate of the indirect teachings of all I have learned and deciphered as my own.

www.asksergeantjen.com

Sergeant Jen says....Let's Talk about Strangers

"Hey Tommy, please hurry! We have to leave!"

"I'm coming, I'm coming…wait a minute" replied the boy smiling. "Here I am, let's go."

"All right, let's go. I was starting to think you weren't coming" said Brandon, teasing his friend.

"No, I really like school and happy that we all walk together in the morning. It's just that I couldn't find one of my books and I was searching everywhere for it. But I finally found it under my book bag" replied Tommy with a smile. "It's all right Tommy, there's no need to explain. We understand, don't we Melissa?"

"For sure Brandon. Hey, you guys did you do the math homework? There was a lot of it, huh?"

"Yes, wow, it seems that Mr. Greenfield must have gotten his kicks giving us that much homework.

But, my mom says it's for our own good" said Tommy.

"Yeah, you're right, Tommy. Even though we may not like it, Mr. Greenfield's homework is necessary. And yes, I did mine. Did you do yours?"

"That homework was kind of hard but eventually I figured it out and did every one of the problems" replied Melissa.

"Yeah they were hard but I'm glad you figured them out" added Brandon.

"Well, it was the only thing I *could* do or else Mr. Greenfield would have given me a "beautiful D-." Because we know, that's what he gives you if you don't do your homework" replied the girl smiling.

"She's right. And my mom would kill me if I got a D- for not doing my homework" said Tommy. "I'd be grounded for a year!"

The children continued their walk toward the school, laughing and chatting the entire way. Before they knew it, they were standing on the sidewalk in front of the school. Together they went inside and headed to their classroom. Most of their classmates were already sitting at their desks, chatting about this and that. The four of them each went to their own desk.

"Oh, school sweet school! I'm so glad it's Monday!" said Tommy.

"Yes, me too Tommy, just not quite as happy as you are" agreed Brandon and smiled.

A few minutes later,
Mr. Greenfield entered the room. He put his books on the table and said: "Good morning, children."

"Good morning, Mr. Greenfield" replied the children.

"How are you all today? Is everything all right?" asked the teacher as he took his seat.

"Yes, Mr. Greenfield" replied the children.

"Very well. Today we have a special guest coming to our classroom. She is a Police Sergeant and her name is Sergeant Jennifer Smith"

"Why is the Sergeant here, Mr. Greenfield? Is one of us in trouble?" asked one of the children.

"No, no. She is here to teach you an important lesson" replied the teacher goodheartedly.

"The Sergeant is going to teach us a lesson?" asked Mary.

"Yes, that's right. She will. And if I'm not mistaken, she should be here soon…" replied the teacher as he looked at the clock on the wall.

"Wow! This is so cool! We having a real Police Sergeant coming to our classroom today!" said some of the children.

"Children, please, please! Be quiet! We don't want the Sergeant to come and find some very noisy kids, do we? So please, let's keep it quiet"

"Yes, Mr. Greenfield. Sorry"

A few minutes later a knock was heard at the door.

"Come in, please" said Mr. Greenfield.

The door opened and a young lady in a Police Sergeant's uniform stepped in. She was very pretty and polite.

"Hello, and good morning. I am Sergeant Jennifer Smith. But I like to be called Sergeant Jen."

"Hello Sergeant Jen" said the teacher shaking her hand." We are very happy to have you here."

"Thank you Mr. Greenfield. I'm happy to be here" replied the Sergeant smiling.

"These are my students" said Mr. Greenfield while looking toward them.

"It's nice to meet all of you" Sergeant Jen said to the class.

"Children, as the Sergeant talks to you about today's lesson, please be polite, say your name, and then you may ask your question. OK?"

"Yes Mr. Greenfield."

"Perfect. You are all wonderful children" added the teacher smiling. "Sergeant Jen, you can start with your lesson and I'll just go sit at one of the empty desks in the back of the classroom. Ok?"

"Yes Mr. Greenfield, thank you."

"You are welcome and enjoy."

"Thank you Sir" replied the woman as she watched the teacher walk towards the desk.

"All right, children. Today we have a very truthful and interesting lesson. It's called "Sergeant Jen says…Let's Talk About Strangers." Now, to start, let's see who a stranger is and is not. Does anyone know who is a stranger?" asked the Sergeant while looking toward the children.

Tommy raised his hand.

"Yes, please"

Tommy spoke and said, "My name is Tommy and a stranger is a person that we don't know."

"That's right, thank you" replied Sergeant Jen smiling. "Yes, a stranger is a person with whom we have no connection whatsoever with and we do not know. They're not your sister or brother. They're not your mother or father. They're people. People that you don't know very well or you don't know at all.

Strangers can be scary, or nice, or pretty. They can be young or old, tall or short, fat or skinny. They can be a man or a woman. There isn't one picture of a stranger that I can show you. Do you know what to do if a stranger talks to you or calls you over??" the Sergeant said kindly. The children looked at each other not quite knowing what to say.

"The answer is you play the "what-if" game *before* that happens so you'll know exactly what to do" said Sergeant Jen.

One of the children raised their hand.

"Yes please, I'm Andy and I want to know what is the "what-if" game?"

"Thank you for asking Andy. I'll explain." said Sergeant Jen goodheartedly. "The best way to keep yourself or your friends safe is to have a plan.

The plan teaches you how to handle a stranger, or any other situation. I call it the "what-if" game and it works like this:

1. What if – someone says they're lost and wants to know if you can show them the way to Main Street, or the ice cream parlor, or the store? The answer is you stand back and tell them you'll get an adult who can help them.

2. What if – a young child runs up to you and says 'My daddy's hurt, come quick.' "What would

you do?" The answer is you tell the child that you'll get an adult who can help.

3. What if - a pretty lady says her cat is lost and needs your help finding her? "Would you help her?" No, you stand back and say that you'll get an adult who can help.

4. What if a man or a woman has a cast on their leg or is in a wheel chair or on crutches and says they need your help opening their van door? "What would you do?" You back far away and go get help from an adult you know."

"Does everyone follow me? So, the game is you imagine different situations in which one stranger would talk to you. How would you answer them? What would you do? This game may seem silly but it's very effective and extremely important" said the Sergeant.

"Sergeant Jen, may I ask you something?" said Sam, Brandon's friend.

"Yes, please."

"My name is Sam and I want to know when we should play this game."

"Good question Sam. You can play it whenever you want. There are no rules about it. The most important thing is that you actually play it."

"Play it when you're walking home, or when you walk to school, when you're on the bus, or when you walk to a friend's house or play in the park. Play it all the time and you will learn what to do if a stranger comes up to you. The more you play, the better you'll get at knowing exactly what to do."

Sergeant Jen went on, "I like playing this game too and I do it pretty often" she said smiling. But she noticed that children put on a surprised face when hearing this. "What? You think an adult shouldn't protect themselves from strangers?" she added kindly.

"Well, you are an adult and you wear a gun. A stranger wouldn't dare hurt you, would he?" said Tommy.

"This is not quite true. Adults must know how to protect themselves from strangers too. It doesn't matter that we are grown ups and can take care of ourselves or children who can't. We should always beware of strangers, because we never know how a situation might end up. So it's always good to pay attention to the details and be careful. Alright?"

"Sergeant Jen, I have a question."

"OK. What's your name?"

"Melissa"

"Melissa, what a beautiful name…! So, what is your question?"

"You said we should pay attention to details. What did you mean by that?"

"Great question Melissa, thank you. Paying attention to the details means noticing the surroundings, what is said, what people are wearing, anything unusual about them and what their face looks like.

For instance, when you came to school this morning, did you notice what your friend was wearing? This could be valuable information in the event of an emergency.

You see children bad people can use all kinds of ways to get you to go with them. They can be very tricky but you can be smarter than them. They can say your mom or dad sent them to pick you up, or they're lost or their dog is lost. A young child may say his mommy or daddy is hurt.

All of these situations won't matter if you've already learned how to deal with them and what to do, ok?"

"It's the best way not to be scared if something does happen. If you practice enough, you'll know a "what-if" situation if it happens to you or one of your friends. When you are prepared, the strangers will see that you're smart and that you're not going to be fooled." said Sergeant Jen.

Another thing you need to know is "the secret word or phrase."

"I like secrets!" said one of the boys in the back of the room.

"What is your name?" Sergeant Jen asked.

"Teddy, Teddy Whitehall."

"Well Teddy, the secret word is not like any secret you've ever known. This secret word could save your life. It works like this.

When you go home tonight, talk to your mom and dad and tell them that there needs to be a secret word or phrase. This word or phrase will only be given to an outsider in the event of an emergency."

Sergeant Jen could see that she had the class, as well as Mr. Greenfield, sitting on the edge of their seats, wondering what she was going to say next.

"Let's say a police officer came up to you and said, "Teddy, you need to come with me, your mom has been hurt." Now, most kids would go with the officer, but you are all too smart for that. Step back and ask, "What's the secret word?" or "What's the secret phrase?" If they don't know it....RUN!!!!!"

"Tell your mom and dad not to ever forget the word and to only use it in emergencies. Oh, and one other thing, you cannot tell any of your friends what the word is. You must keep this a secret between you and your parents."

"You cannot tell anyone. Not a teacher, not a pastor, not a police officer, no one. Also, if you have a brother or sister, the secret word should be different for each of you."

"My husband and I have a secret word also. If anyone does anything that raises our suspicion, we will ask what the secret word is. Does everyone understand how important this is? The word you and your parents come up with could save your life."

"All right, let's move to the next topic now..."

While the Sergeant was talking, Brandon thought about what she had said. He was amazed. Not even once did he ever think about something like this. No, it was quite silly and this was only for small children. He would never play the "what-if" game; that was for sure.

Everyone he knows is so nice and friendly, why would he ever play this stupid game? No, definitely, the game was not for him. He was sure about that. Let the others play the game, but not him. He didn't need a secret word. He would never go with anyone so why bother? No, Brandon thought that all of this was pure nonsense. While Brandon's thoughts were racing, he was only half-hearing the rest of the lesson.

The Sergeant showed them how to walk in the middle of the sidewalk, how to pay attention to their surroundings, and how to use the "buddy" system. The children were so excited about everything Sergeant Jen had taught them. Especially Sam! He was crazy about the "what-if" game and had already started playing it. It was a great source of amusement for him.

When school was over, the four friends were heading toward home. On the way, they talked about today's lesson, about the Sergeant as well as everything else that they learned in class. Tommy, Sam and Melissa were so excited and they couldn't help but talk about it. They were all chattering at the same time about Sergeant Jen's lesson. The only quiet one was Brandon. He kept quiet, leaving his three friends talking and laughing about everything.

"Hey Brandon, what wrong?"

"About what, Sam?"

"You're so quiet. Ever since we left school we've been talking about what Sergeant Jen taught us and you haven't said anything about it. It really was a great class. Didn't you like it?"

"Well…yes, a little. It's just that I don't think what the Sergeant told us will ever happen to me. I can't believe that it's possible for me to ever have to deal with a stranger like that" replied Brandon.

"What makes you say that? You never know" said Melissa.

"I know. But still, I find it hard to believe. I have always seen myself as being a strong boy, a boy who can manage all possible situations. That is why I find it rather stupid to play that silly "what-if" game" said Brandon while looking at his friends.

"But you heard Sergeant Jen. She plays the game herself, even though she's an adult"

"Yes, I heard her. You don't need to remind me Tommy."

"Hey Brandon, what if an alien wanted to shoot you with his space gun?" asked Sam. The rest of the group burst out laughing. "Hey guys, stop laughing! This could really happen!" added Sam seriously.

"Only in your dreams, Sam. Everyone knows there's no such thing as aliens!" said Tommy laughing.

"How can you tell, Tommy? Is this something you can be sure of?"

"Well…no, but still…Hey, it's a fact that aliens don't exist" replied Tommy.

"Hey, guys, guys, please. This is not the point, really. The issue is with Brandon. He says he won't play the "what-if" game because he thinks it's silly. I wish you would play it with us, Brandon. You never know and I don't want to hear that you went through a situation like this with a stranger and didn't know what to do" said Melissa looking at him.

"Melissa, I understand. But that's not the case, really. I can handle any situation with a stranger even if I won't play that game."

"Brandon, what if someone grabbed you, what would you do"? asked Sam all of a sudden.

"Sam, I am the oldest and that would never happen" replied Brandon.

"But what if you're walking on the street and a lady calls out to you to help her catch a mouse in her house? Would you go?"

"Sam, I've already answered, I am the oldest and that would never happen."

"But still, would you go?" insisted the boy.

"Sam…"

"Would you, Brandon?" asked Melissa looking straight into his eyes.

"Not you too, Melissa…."

"But it's important, Brandon. Stop being so full of yourself and face it! It could happen to you too!"

"Well, I don't believe it could ever happen!"

"That just means you are living in a fantasy world! If this couldn't happen to any of us, then I guess that Sergeant Jen wouldn't have bothered to come to our school and teach us about all these things, would she?" said Melissa.

"Melissa is right, Brandon" agreed Tommy.

"Still…"

"Why are you so stubborn, Brandon? Surely it could happen to any of us" said Sam.

"I'm not stubborn…it's just how I see things, that's all" replied Brandon. "Well anyway, let's get going, shall we? Our moms are probably waiting for us"

"Yes, we better get going. Hey Tommy, if a man gives me a dollar to go get him a drink, should I do it"?

"Absolutely not. What if the man grabbed me as he was giving me the dollar"? "Come on Sammy…..think".

These questions were asked and answered by each other, but somehow, Sergeant Jen's voice stayed in the back of all their minds.

Then Melissa looked up and said, "Brandon, can we at least have a secret word…just for the four of us? You know, in case we need it?"

Brandon looked at Melissa and could see that she was really concerned. "Sure, let's have a secret word. But we cannot tell anyone and we can only use it in an emergency. Does anyone have a word?"

"Ooo…..Ooo, I do I do" said Sam. "What about 'aliens'?"

"That's stupid" said Tommy. "Anyone who knows you could guess that word. You love space anything!"

Words like 'baseball', 'happy', 'school', and others were tossed around by the boys.

Melissa was looking down as they walked and said, "purple cow."

"That's dumb" said Sam. "Purple cow? Moooooo" said Tommy.

"No, wait" said Brandon. "It's not one word, it's two. Purple is Melissa's favorite color. And 'cow'? Why not?"

The boys all looked at each other, then at Melissa. "Ok Melissa, 'purple cow' it is" said Sam.

♠♠♠

Several months later on a beautiful Saturday morning, Brandon asked his mom if he could go to the park. He told her that Tommy, Sam and Melissa were all going to be there. She agreed but only after he finished his chores.

Brandon made his bed, fed the dog, took out the garbage and swept the front porch and sidewalk. After finishing his chores his mom told him to go play at the park.

When he got to the park the rest of his friends were already there. The gang was complete: Brandon, Tommy, Sam and Melissa. They had a great time playing and running among the trees. They swung on the swing set, went up and down on the seesaw. They were laughing and joking joyfully and everyone who saw them play couldn't help but smile.

"Hey guys, wait for me!" said Sam while throwing himself down and rolling over the green grass. Wow! What a run!"

"And what a day, too!" said Tommy." Hey, where is Melissa?"

"Oh there she is, at the fountain" replied Sam. "She getting a drink of water"

"Oh, all right. Let's wait for her and then go home? I'm pretty hungry, what do you guys say?" said Brandon as he held his stomach and moaned.

"Me too. I'm starving!"

"Sam, you are always hungry. No news in that" Tommy joked.

"Well yes, but still…today I'm even hungrier because I ran so much!" said he smiling. So I need food now"

"Oh Sammy, you're really something. Such drama." added Brandon laughing as well.

Melissa finished her drink and joined them. "Hey guys, what's going on?" she said the girl while sitting down on the grass next to Sam.

"We're just waiting for you so that we can go home and get something to eat. We're all pretty hungry" said Tommy.

"Me, too. I could eat a sandwich" said Melissa.

"Then it's settled, let's go" said Brandon as he too got up from the grass. The four of them were so tired they decided not to run, but walk home.

"I'm so glad its Saturday. We have the entire day off!"

"Don't forget about the homework, Tommy. You don't want to go to school on Monday without it done, would you?" said Melissa teasing him.

"No I wouldn't" replied Tommy as he winked at her.

"Hey, how about all of you come to my house and we'll do our homework together? I'll ask my mom to make us some pizza. What do you say?" Brandon said with excitement in his voice.

"I think it's a great idea Brandon. Yeah, let's do it! I don't think my mom would say no."

"So Sammy is in. What about you two?"

"Let me know the time and I'll be there" replied Tommy.

"Perfect. And you Melissa?"

"I will have to ask my mom first but I think she will let me come. What time do you want us there Brandon?"

"Hmm, how about 6pm? And if we finish with all our homework, we'll have tomorrow free and we can play all day!"

"Brilliant plan Brandon! Let's do this!" said Sammy.

"I totally agree" added Brandon smiling. "I am glad you all agreed with my 'brilliant' idea"

"Well, it's a pretty good one. The best idea you've had in a long time" added Tommy, smiling while giving Brandon an elbow to the side.

"Thanks."

Then, a female voice interrupted them.

"Children, may I ask you something? I apologize for bothering you" said the lady.

All four of them turned toward the woman.

"Yes, of course Ma'am. Can we help you with something?"

"Well, it would be terrific if you could but let me tell you first what's happened. You see I have a little dog, her name is Muffin and I've lost her. I have this picture of her" said the woman as she pulled a small picture out of her purse. "By any chance have any of you seen Muffin?" she added.

Each child looked at the picture but the dog wasn't familiar to any of them.

"No, sorry Ma'am. I haven't seen your dog." Tommy said.

"Me neither" added Sam.

"Me neither" said Melissa and Brandon.

"Oh well, I understand. It's all right, really" said the woman on a disappointed tone." I love my little dog very much and would be so relieved if I could find Muffin and have her back with me where she belongs. She's going to be so scared if I don't find her before dark. Would you please be kind enough to help me look for her?" the woman asked politely.

The kids looked at each other.

"I mean, at least one of you. I know it would probably be too much for all four of you to come" added the woman while eyeing them. The children still looked at each other, as if they would have talked through their looks. Eventually,

Melissa stepped forward, forgetting about the sandwich she wanted, and said:

"Oh, alright, I'll help you. I don't want your dog to be scared."

"Oh, thank you so much sweetheart. This is so generous of you, thank you" said the woman. "If you don't mind, my car is a bit further from here; let's go and try to find Muffin, ok?"

Just as the woman grabbed Melissa by the arm, Brandon grabbed Melissa's hand.

"She can't go with you".

Brandon knew this was a "what-if" situation.

"What if?" whispered Tommy.

"Definitely "what if" added Sam.

"Melissa can't go with you."

"Remember what Sergeant Jen taught us" said Brandon to Tommy and Sam. "Melissa, you can't go with her!"

"Hey, boy, what's the matter with you? Melissa said she wants to come with me to help find Muffin. What's wrong with that?" said the woman with loud and irritated voice.

Brandon pulled Melissa towards him. The woman grew angry and screamed at Brandon. "What are you doing? I need her help."

Tommy piped up and said, "We'll go get an adult to help you."

"No! What adult? No way! I just want her!" replied the woman furiously.

At that moment, Sam and Tommy stood between the woman and Melissa. Tommy whispered to Melissa:

"Purple cow!"

She nodded.

"RUN!!" yelled Tommy.

Melissa ran and yelled "Stranger! Stranger! Help, there's a stranger!"

Luckily, Mr. Wells quickly came out of his store and looked directly at the woman.

"Hey you! Come here!"

The woman turned and ran down the street and around the corner. She dropped the photo of the puppy. Mr. Wells called the police and several minutes later, they arrived.

"Good afternoon Mr. Wells. You called us." said one of the officers.

"Yes, yes I have, officer. It seems that these children had some problems with a woman but now she gone.

"It's all right, Mr. Wells. We will find her. Children, can you tell us what happened?" said the second officer.

"Well, a woman came up to us and asked whether we had seen her dog, Muffin. We said no but then she asked if we could help her find the dog. Melissa at first said she would help, but I told the lady that Melissa couldn't help her. She wanted Melissa to go to her car with her. When I grabbed Melissa's hand, the lady tried to take Melissa by force, saying she wanted her to help her find the dog. Then the lady got really mad when Tommy told her he would get an adult to help her. We whispered the secret word to Melissa and that's when Melissa ran and started screaming "Stranger! Stranger!" And then, Mr. Wells came out of his store and yelled at the lady." said Brandon completely out of breath and a bit shaken.

"Here's the picture of her lost dog. She dropped it when she ran" said Tommy as he handed it to the officer.

"Thank you. Can you kids tell us what she looked like?"

"Oh yes! Yes! I know" said Sam as he squeezed pass Brandon, Tommy and Melissa. "I know. I know what she had on. She was wearing red shoes and had on a blue coat. Her hair was brown and down to here" said Sammy as he pointed at Melissa's lower back, "but it was in a pony tail." "Oh, and she had a cut on her…wait"

He turned his little body in the direction the lady was standing:

"This hand, here on her hand." Sam pointed to his right hand. "Oh, and she had blue eyes".

"Thank you, little one. This is very helpful said the officer. "OK kids, I think we have enough information. We're going to circle the area and see if we can find her."

Then he turned and got in the police car along with the other officer.

Tommy turned to Sam and said, "Blue eyes? How do you know all this?"

"Well in class, Sergeant Jen said to try to remember what the person looks like and what they are wearing. She also said to try to remember something special, not just the color of their hair. So while you and Brandon were looking after Melissa, I looked at the lady" replied Sam smiling.

Brandon ruffled Sam's hair and said:

"Good job! Sergeant Jen would be so proud of you."

"Thanks Brandon. I am just happy that I remembered all her words and that Melissa is ok." "That's right, Sam. You're a good friend.

"Oh Tommy, thank you for saying the secret word" Melissa said. "And thank you, Sam" as she gently kissed him on his cheek.

Sam wiped the kiss off, but that didn't stop Brandon and Tommy from teasing him.

♠♠♠

Meanwhile, the two officers drove around several blocks and soon they spotted a woman talking to a young boy on the sidewalk near the park. She was wearing red shoes but she didn't have on a coat. The lady was holding something in her hand as she was talking to the boy.

The police officers got out of their police car and walked toward her. As they came closer, they heard her asking the boy to help her find her lost cat.

"Good afternoon, Miss. Can we ask what you are doing here?" said one of them.

The woman looked surprised.

"Officers...How lovely you've come! I could use your help, officers."

"Really? Why is that, Miss?"

"Oh, you are so kind! You see, I have this cat, her name is Fluffy and I've lost her. I was just asking this little boy if he had seen her. I love my cat and want so much to find her. So can you help me? I'd really appreciate it" said the woman smiling.

"Yes, I bet you would" said the first officer. "It would be the same for your lost dog also?" said the second officer when noticing the cut on her hand. That's when he knew it was the same woman Sam had described.

"Dog? What dog, officer? I don't know anything about a dog. I only have a cat. Surely you must be mistaking me for someone else." replied the lady acting surprised.

"Put the handcuffs on her, Chuck. We have our person."

"With pleasure Robert. Miss, you are under arrest. Anything you say can and will be used against you."

"What? But I didn't do anything! What's this all about? Is this some kind of a joke? Let me go!"

"You're not going anywhere. We're taking you down to the police station for questioning. Let's go"

"No! This is not fair! I'm not a criminal!" said the woman but the officers would not listen. The officers were going to find out exactly why she wanted to take children with her and if there were other children that she may have grabbed.

Officers Chuck and Robert thought how prepared Brandon, Tommy, Sam, and Melissa were and that by them having a plan they possibly prevented something bad from happening.

"I wish all children would have a well thought-out plan like those kids did", Officer Chuck said. "Then maybe there would be fewer criminals on the streets".

The End

www.ingramcontent.com/pod-product-compliance
Lightning Source LLC
Chambersburg PA
CBHW041745040426
42444CB00004B/182